GoWISE USA Air Fryer Cookbook for Beginners

Fast, Easy and Healthy Air Fryer Recipes For Everyone

Bruce Boone

Copyright © 2018 by Bruce Boone

All rights reserved worldwide.

ISBN: 978-1980891093

No part of this book may be reproduced or transmitted in any form or by any means, electronic or mechanical, including photocopying, recording or by any information storage and retrieval system, without written permission from the publisher, except for the inclusion of brief quotations in a review.

Warning-Disclaimer

The purpose of this book is to educate and entertain. The author or publisher does not guarantee that anyone following the techniques, suggestions, tips, ideas, or strategies will become successful. The author and publisher shall have neither liability or responsibility to anyone with respect to any loss or damage caused, or alleged to be caused, directly or indirectly by the information contained in this book.

Contents

Introduction 8

Pre-Set Programs of GoWISE USA Air Fryer 9

Breakfast Recipes 13

Breakfast Muffins 13

Rarebit 13

Ham and Cheese Mini Quiche 14

Breakfast Banana Bread 15

Chorizo Spanish Frittata 15

Cinnamon Toast 16

Baked Kale Omelet 17

Breakfast Sandwich 17

Air Fried Hash Browns 18

Spicy Egg and Bacon Wraps 19

Flaxseed Porridge 19

Lunch Recipes 20

Caprese on Toast 20

Mac and Cheese 20

Air Fried Calzone 21

Roasted Radish and Onion Cheesy Salad 22

Yogurt Garnished Minty Meatballs 23

Melty and Gooey Chicken Sandwich 24

Mock Stir Fry 25

Prosciutto and Mozzarella Bruschetta 26

Potato and Bacon Salad 26

Side Dishes and Snacks 27

Air Fried Potatoes Au Gratin 27

Cheesy Prosciutto Croquettes 28

Air Fried Pickles 28

Sweet Mascarpone Figs 29

Grilled Lime Corn 30

Mozzarella Cheese Sticks 30

Veggie Ham Rolls with Cashew Nuts 31

Cauliflower Buffalo 32

Air Fried Bananas 32

Pigs in Blankets 33

Chorizo Empanadas 34

Air Fried Potatoes with Eggs and Cheese 34

Potato Chips Creamy Dip 35

Pumpkin Ham Fritters 36

Parmesan and Garlic French Fries 36

Salty and Vinegary Zucchini Chips 37

Poultry Recipes 38

Buffalo Chicken 38

Pineapple Chicken 38

Crunchy Chicken Fingers 39

Air Fried Chicken with Black Beans 40

Quick and Crispy Chicken 40

Chicken with Rice 41

Mustard and Maple Turkey Breast 42

Air Fried Chicken with Honey and Lemon 43

Chicken Breasts with Tarragon 44

Cajun Chicken Tenders 44

Chicken with Cashew Nuts 45

Crunchy Coconut Chicken 46

Air Fried Southern Drumsticks 46

Fried Chicken Legs 47

Turkey Cordon Bleu 48

Beef, Pork and Lamb Recipes 49

Roast Beef 49

Healthier Burgers 49

Meatballs in Tomato Sauce 50

Liver Soufflé 51

Air Fried Beef Empanada 51

Liver Muffins with Eggs 52

The Simples and Yummiest Rib Eye Steak 53

Panko Beef Schnitzel 53

Beef Bulgogi 54

The Ultimate Beef Chili 55

Vegetarian Recipes 56

Nutty Pumpkin with Blue Cheese 56

Eggplant Cheeseburger 57

Veggie Meatballs 58

Crunchy Parmesan Zucchini 59

Chili Bean Burritos 59

Spinach and Feta Crescent Triangles 60

Feta Cheese Triangles 61

Cheesy Broccoli with Eggs 62

Eggplant Caviar 62

Ratatouille 63

Chile Relleno 64

Cabbage Steaks 64

Vegetable Spring Rolls 65

Cheesy Spinach Enchiladas 66

Cheesy Muffins 66

Stuffed Garlicky Mushrooms 67

Stuffed Mushrooms 68

Cauliflower Rice 68

Air Fried Vegetables with Garlic 69

Fish and Seafood Recipes 70

Frozen sesame Fish Fillets 70

Air Fried Dilly Salmon 71

Air Fried Calamari 71

Flatten Salmon Balls 72

Fish Tacos 73

Sautéed Shrimp 73

Peppery and Lemony Haddock 74

Soy Sauce Glazed Cod 75

Salmon Cakes 75

Rosemary Garlic Prawns 76

Dessert Recipes 77

Soft Buttermilk Biscuits 77

Orange Sponge Cake 78

Lemon Glazed Muffins 79

Mock Cherry Pie 80

Simple Coffee Cake 80

Berry Crumble 81

Banana Fritters 82

Baked apples 82

Pecan Pie 83

Introduction

Million people around the world challenge themselves whether they should eat healthy food or tasty food. Obviously, it is important to care about your health in order to live long and happy life. But would you be happy without delicious meals? Tasty food brings us a feeling of satisfaction and joy, which are extremely important for individuals. GoWise USA has a solution to this age-old problem by a genius invention – the Air Fryer. The Air Fryer helps to cook wholesome dinner with adding a minimum amount of oil or even no oil at all.

Are you fan of French fries, fried chicken, tater tots or a juicy steak with a crispy crust? These products are not considered to be healthy meal options, especially if you buy them at a fast food restaurant. However, these foods can be healthier if you cook them at home with the Air Fryer. Rather than drowning these foods in boiling oil, your favorite kind of fried potato can be prepared in a one spoon of oil! New technologies like this have changed the world of culinary, and now you can have all of the benefits in your home. Your meals will taste richer, while the number of extra calories and harmful fats you consume will decrease significantly.

Even if you think that your culinary skills are not that great, you can cook like a chef using this modern kitchen appliance. Our cooking book will acquaint you with the world of simple, but super delicious meals that you can cook in the fastest and the easiest way. You will be amazed when you will cook your dinner in the Air Fryer for a first time. When you put a piece of roasted potato into your mouth, you will fall in love with the combination of crispy edges and tender creamy interior.

Has your mouth started watering yet? It's time to start a fun culinary journey and learn about all advantages of GoWise USA Air Fryer!

Pre-Set Programs of GoWISE USA Air Fryer

Depending on the model, there are 7 or 8 pre-set modes.

- **Pork**. This program will help you to prepare juicy pork with an amazing crispy crust without adding tons of fats.

- **Chips**. Fast, home-made snacks have an ideal taste when cooked in this program.

- **Fish**. Your favorite type of fish cooks fast in this program. Whether it is a salmon or tuna, it will be prepared perfectly and melt in your mouth.

- **Chicken**. Poultry such as turkey, chicken breasts, and wings can be prepared in this program. They will remain tender on the inside, but crunchy outside.

- **Steak**. It can be pretty difficult to cook a perfect steak, but everything become easier with the Air Fryer. This mode will help you to prepare yummy steak of any degree of doneness from rare to well.

- **Shrimp**. If you like fried seafood like including shrimp and calamari, you should be cooking them using this specifically design program for healthier, delicious bites everytime.

- **Cake**. Do you have some baking experience? Even if you have never made a cake before, you can follow a simple recipe, choose this mode and be ready to taste delicious homemade dessert in an hour or less.

- **Warm**. Crunchy food tastes better, when it's hot. If your crispy dinner is ready, but you want to eat it later, just turn this mode to prevent cooling.

Tasty and Wholesome Meals

Health must be a number one priority, so it is really important to start building better eating habits right now. First step is to give up eating processed food and fast food and to start cooking at home. Ready-to-eat products always contain hidden sodium, sugar, trans-fats, preservatives and colorants. When you consume enormous amounts of them, you do not even notice what it is doing to your body until you are very unhealthy.

By cooking at home and using high-quality, natural ingredients, we can ensure that our nutrition is "clean" and wholesome. The Air Fryer is a great kitchen appliance that helps you prepare healthy foods without any specific efforts. Even if you will use the Air Fryer to cook the same dishes that you have always cooked, you will significantly decrease the amount of oil and, consequently, cut your daily calorie intake. This small change will help you to normalize the cholesterol level and benefit your body.

New Way of Healthy Eating

The hardest thing about diets is the absolute restriction of some kinds of yummy food. As a result, most of people find it impossible to stick to the diet all the time and just give it up. However, more and more nutritionists offer to use 80/20 rule: 80% of all calorie intake should come from the dietary products, and 20% from any kind of food you like. In such a way you will be able to enjoy your favorite food while you are working on your fitness goals.

It means that if you adore fried chips, you can still eat them when you control the portion size. Moreover, all chips and French fries, which you can cook at home with GoWise USA Air Fryer, are considered as a wholesome alternative to the products from the supermarket shelves. Being guided by 80/20 rule, you can satisfy your needs for goodies, feel happy, and have a strong mental and physical health.

Capacity Options

Keep in mind that the GoWise USA Air Fryer is available in two different capacities: 3.7 quart and 5.8 quart. The smaller one is perfect for a couple, and the second one is ideal for families. Depending on the volume of your meals, you should choose the capacity that meets your needs the best.

Easy to Clean

The cleaning process is as easy as the cooking process. All of the parts of the appliance that have any contact with the food are removable. Each of them can be washed in dishwashing machine. The appliance by itself with its heating elements and wires should be cleaned with a clean, damp sponge.

Time Saving

As a rule, cooking is very time-consuming process. That is why so many people find it easier to eat unhealthy fast food. With GoWise USA Air Fryer, you will learn a new way of meal preparation, which is much faster and more joyful than ordinary cooking. When you want to cook crispy chips, you do not need to stand next to the pot of boiling oil and to dream about escaping from your kitchen. From now, you only need to put all ingredients in removable food tray and close the lid – Air Fryer will do all the rest for you. It means that you will be able not only establish healthier eating habits, but also spend more time on things you need to or rather be doing.

Keep Your Place Fresh

When you cook with the Air Fryer, you avoid few unpleasant issues such as an unpleasant smell of the burning oil, the noise, and extra heat from the oil fryer or oven. All smells will be locked in the pot, so your kitchen will remain fresh. The Air Fryer is quiet, so it will not disturb the peace of your home with the irritating sounds. In contrast to an ordinary oven, this new kind of kitchen appliance doesn't emit a lot of heat. It means, that even during the hot summer you will be able to maintain a comfortable temperature in your kitchen.

5 Simple Steps to Prepare Your Dinner

1. **Choose the recipe.** If you are newbie at cooking with the Air Fryer, it is a great idea to follow the recipe step by step. It will ensure that your first dish will be really tasty. Make sure that you have all of the necessary ingredients, and do not forget about salt, sugar, pepper etc.

2. **Prepare all ingredients according to the recipe.** Sometimes you need to wash ingredients, cut them, or make some marinade, if it is required. Another important note: make sure that all products are absolutely dry. This is because any excess water will break down the cooking process.

3. **Remove the food tray.** Take a food tray away from the machine, fill it with the ingredients, then put it back.

4. **Start the program.** Touch the LCD display and choose an appropriate program or utilize manual settings.

5. **Serve dinner.** As soon as Air Fryer stops cooking, you can take the food away from the tray. It is time for you can enjoy your delicious and healthy meal.

Breakfast Recipes

Breakfast Muffins

(Prep + Cook Time: 15 minutes / Servings: 4)

Nutritional info per serving:

Calories 214.1, Carbohydrates 24.3 g, Fat 12.7 g, Protein 2.7 g

Ingredients:

1 cup flour	1 tsp. chopped walnuts
¼ cup mashed banana	½ tsp. baking powder
¼ cup powdered sugar	¼ cup oats
1 tsp. milk	¼ cup butter, room temperature

Directions:

1. Preheat the air fryer to 320 degrees F.
2. Place the sugar, walnuts, banana, and butter in a bowl and mix to combine.
3. In another bowl, combine the flour, baking powder and oats.
4. Combine the two mixtures together, and stir in the milk.
5. Grease a muffin tin and pour the batter in. Place it into the Air Fryer.
6. Bake 10 minutes and serve hot.

Rarebit

(Prep + Cook Time: 15 minutes / Servings: 2)

Nutritional info per serving:

Calories 401.5, Carbohydrates 15.4 g, Fat 27.2 g, Protein 26.9 g

Ingredients:

3 slices of bread
1 tsp. smoked paprika
2 eggs

1 tsp. Dijon mustard
4 ½ oz. cheddar cheese, grated
Salt and pepper, to taste

Directions:

1. Toast the bread in the air fryer to your liking. In a bowl, whisk the eggs.
2. Stir in the mustard, cheddar and paprika. Season with some salt and pepper.
3. Spread the mixture on the toasts.
4. Cook the bread slices for about 10 minutes at 360 degrees F.

Ham and Cheese Mini Quiche

(Prep + Cook Time: 30 minutes / Servings: 8)

Nutritional info per serving:

Calories 365.7, Carbohydrates 21.4 g, Fat 20.4 g, Protein 8.9 g

Ingredients:

1 shortcrust pastry
3 oz. chopped ham
½ tcup grated cheese
4 eggs, beaten

3 tbsp. Greek yogurt
¼ tsp. garlic powder
¼ tsp. salt
¼ tsp. black pepper

Directions:

1. Preheat the air fryer to 330 degrees F.
2. Take 8 ramekins and sprinkle them with flour to avoid sticking.
3. Cut the shortcrust pastry into 8 equal pieces to make 8 mini quiches.
4. Line the ramekins with the pastry.
5. Combine all of the other ingredients in a bowl.
6. Divide the filling between the ramekins. Cook for 20 minutes.

Breakfast Banana Bread

(Prep + Cook Time: 50 minute / Servings: 2)

Nutritional info per serving:

Calories 438, Carbohydrates 58 g, Fat 21 g, Protein 7.6 g

Ingredients:

1 cup plus 1 tbsp. flour
¼ tsp. baking soda
1 tsp. baking powder
⅓ cup sugar
2 mashed bananas
¼ cup vegetable oil

1 egg, beaten
1 tsp. vanilla extract
¾ cup chopped walnuts
2 tbsp. peanut butter
2 tbsp. sour cream
Cooking spray or butter for greasing

Directions:

1. Preheat the air fryer to 330 degrees F.
2. Spray a small baking dish with cooking spray or grease with butter.
3. Combine the flour, salt, baking powder, and baking soda in a bowl.
4. In another bowl combine bananas, oil, egg, peanut butter, vanilla, sugar, and sour cream. Combine both mixtures gently. Stir in the chopped walnuts.
5. Pour the batter into the dish. Bake for 40 minutes. Serve cool.

Chorizo Spanish Frittata

(Prep + Cook Time: 12 minutes / Servings: 2)

Nutritional info per serving:

Calories 438.2, Carbohydrates 39.4 g, Fat 22.9 g, Protein 20.4 g

Ingredients:

3 eggs
1 large potato, boiled and cubed

½ cup frozen corn
½ cup feta cheese, crumbled

1 tbsp. chopped parsley
½ chorizo, sliced

3 tbsp. olive oil
Salt and pepper, to taste

Directions:

1. Pour the olive oil into the air fryer and preheat it to 330 degrees F.
2. Cook the chorizo just so it becomes slightly browned.
3. Beat the eggs with some salt and pepper in a bowl.
4. Stir in all of the remaining ingredients.
5. Pour the mixture into the air fryer, give it a stir, and cook for 6 minutes.
6. Enjoy.

Cinnamon Toast

(Prep + Cook Time: 10 minutes / Servings: 6))

Nutritional info per serving:

Calories 342.5, Carbohydrates 39.2 g, Fat 19.3 g, Protein 3.2 g

Ingredients:

12 slices of bread
½ cup sugar
1 ½ tsp. cinnamon

1 stick of butter, softened
1 tsp. vanilla extract

Directions:

1. Preheat the air fryer to 400 degrees F.
2. Combine all of the ingredients except the bread, in a bowl.
3. Spread the buttery cinnamon mixture onto the bread slices.
4. Place the bread slices in the air fryer.
5. Cook for 5 minutes.
6. Served cut diagonally.
7. Enjoy.

Baked Kale Omelet

(Prep + Cook Time: 15 minutes / Servings: 1)

Nutritional info per serving:

Calories 294, Carbohydrates 3.9 g, Fat 19.5 g, Protein 24.7 g

Ingredients:

3 eggs
3 tbsp. cottage cheese
3 tbsp. chopped kale
½ tbsp. chopped basil
½ tbsp. chopped parsley
Salt and pepper, to taste
1 tsp. olive oil

Directions:

1. Add oil to the air fryer and preheat it to 330 degrees F.
2. Beat the eggs with some salt and pepper, in a bowl.
3. Stir in the rest of the ingredients.
4. Pour the mixture into the air fryer and bake for 10 minutes.
5. Enjoy.

Breakfast Sandwich

(Prep + Cook Time: 10 minutes / Servings: 1)

Nutritional info per serving:

Calories 240.7, Carbohydrates 25.5 g, Fat 8.8 g, Protein 13.3 g

Ingredients:

1 egg
1 English muffin
2 slices of bacon
Salt and pepper, to taste

Directions:

1. Preheat the air fryer to 395 degrees.
2. Crack the egg into a ramekin.
3. Place the muffin, egg and bacon in the air fryer.
4. Cook for 6 minutes.
5. Let cool slightly so you can assemble the sandwich. Cut the muffin in half.
6. Place the egg on one half and season with salt and pepper.
7. Arrange the bacon on top.
8. Top with the other muffin half.

Air Fried Hash Browns

(Prep + Cook Time: 20 minutes / Servings: 2)

Nutritional info per serving:

Calories 507, Carbohydrates 74.2 g, Fat 14.8 g, Protein 18.3 g

Ingredients:

1 large potato, grated
3 eggs, beaten
½ tsp. garlic powder
¼ tsp. nutmeg

1 tbsp. olive oil
1 cup flour
Salt and pepper, to taste

Directions:

1. Add the olive oil in the air fryer and heat it to 390 degrees F.
2. In a bowl, combine flour, eggs, potato, nutmeg, and garlic powder.
3. Season with some salt and pepper.
4. Form patties out of the mixture.
5. Arrange in the air fryer and cook for 15 minutes.
6. Enjoy.

Spicy Egg and Bacon Wraps

(Prep + Cook Time: 15 minutes / Servings: 3)

Nutritional info per serving:

Calories 385.4, Carbohydrates 20.1 g, Fat 25.3 g, Protein 17.1 g

Ingredients:

3 tortillas
2 previously scrambled eggs
3 slices bacon, cut into strips
3 tbsp. salsa
3 tbsp. cream cheese, divided
1 cup grated cheese (preferable Pepper Jack)

Directions:

1. Preheat the air fryer to 390 degrees F. Spread one tbsp. of cream cheese onto each tortilla. Divide the eggs and bacon between the tortillas evenly. Top with salsa.
2. Sprinkle some grated cheese over. Roll up the tortillas. Cook for 10 minutes.

Flaxseed Porridge

(Prep + Cook Time: 5 minutes / Servings: 4)

Nutritional info per serving:

Calories 450, Carbohydrates 67 g, Fat 18.9 g, Protein 20.2 g

Ingredients:

2 cups steel cut oats
1 cup flax seeds
1 tbsp. peanut butter
1 tbsp. butter
4 cups milk
4 tbsp. honey

Directions:

1. Preheat the air fryer to 390 degrees F. Combine all of the ingredients in an ovenproof bowl.
2. Place in the air fryer for 5 minutes. Stir and serve with your favorite topping.

Lunch Recipes

Caprese on Toast

(Prep + Cook Time: 7 minutes / Servings: 1)

Nutritional info per serving:

Calories 514, Carbohydrates 24.8 g, Fat 33.3 g, Protein 34.2 g

Ingredients:

2 slices of bread
4 tomato slices
4 mozzarella slices

1 tbsp. olive oil
1 tbsp. chopped basil
Salt and pepper, to taste

Directions:

1. Preheat the air fryer to 370 degrees F.
2. Place the bread slices in the air fryer and toast for 3 minutes.
3. Arrange two tomato slices on each bread slice. Season with salt and pepper.
4. Top each slice with 2 mozzarella slices. Return to the air fryer and cook for 1 minute more.
5. Drizzle the caprese toasts with olive oil and top with chopped basil.

Mac and Cheese

(Prep + Cook Time: 15 minutes / Servings: 2)

Nutritional info per serving:

Calories 375.6, Carbohydrates 23 g, Fat 1.8 g, Protein 6.4 g

Ingredients:

1 cup cooked macaroni

1 cup grated cheddar cheese

½ cup warm milk
1 tbsp. Parmesan cheese

Salt and pepper, to taste

Directions:

1. Preheat the air fryer to 350 degrees F.
2. Add the macaroni to an ovenproof baking dish.
3. Stir in the cheddar and milk. Season with some salt and pepper, to taste.
4. Place the dish in the air fryer and cook for 10 minutes.
5. Sprinkle with Parmesan cheese.

Air Fried Calzone

(Prep + Cook Time: 20 minutes / Servings: 4)

Nutritional info per serving:

Calories 339, Carbohydrates 10.6 g, Fat 17.3 g, Protein 33.6 g

Ingredients:

Pizza dough, preferably homemade
4 oz. cheddar cheese, grated
1 oz. mozzarella cheese
1 oz. bacon, diced
2 cups cooked and shredded turkey
(leftovers are fine)
1 egg, beaten
1 tsp. thyme
4 tbsp. tomato paste
1 tsp. basil
1 tsp. oregano
Salt and pepper, to taste

Directions:

1. Preheat the air fryer to 350 degrees F.
2. Divide the pizza dough into 4 equal pieces so you have dough for 4 small pizza crusts.
3. Combine the tomato paste, basil, oregano, and thyme, in a small bowl.
4. Brush the mixture onto the crusts just make sure not to go all the way and avoid brushing near the edges.

5. On one half of each crust, place ½ turkey, and season the meat with some salt and pepper.
6. Top the meat with some bacon.
7. Combine the cheddar and mozzarella and divide it between the pizzas, making sure that you layer only one half of the dough.
8. Brush the edges of the crust with the beaten egg.
9. Fold the crust and seal with a fork. Cook for 10 minutes.

Roasted Radish and Onion Cheesy Salad

(Prep + Cook Time: 35 minutes / Servings: 4)

Nutritional info per serving:

Calories 240.1, Carbohydrates 9.7 g, Fat 16 g, Protein 15 g

Ingredients:

1 lb. radishes, green parts too
1 large red onion, sliced
½ lb. mozzarella, sliced
2 tbsp. olive oil, plus more for drizzling
2 tbsp. balsamic glaze
1 tsp. dried basil
1 tsp. dried parsley
1 tsp. salt

Directions:

1. Preheat the air fryer to 350 degrees F.
2. Wash the radishes well and dry them by patting with paper towels.
3. Cut them in half and place in a large bowl.
4. Add the onion slices in. Stir in salt, basil, parsley and olive oil.
5. Place in the basket of the air fryer. Cook for 30 minutes.
6. Make sure to toss them twice while cooking. Stir in the mozzarella immediately so that it begins to melt.
7. Stir in the balsamic glaze. Drizzle with olive oil.

Yogurt Garnished Minty Meatballs

(Prep + Cook Time: 22 minutes / Servings: 4)

Nutritional info per serving:

Calories 578, Carbohydrates 5.3 g, Fat 47.9 g, Protein 30.4 g

Ingredients:

Meatballs:

1 ½ tbsp. chopped parsley
1 lb. ground lamb
4 oz. ground turkey
1 tbsp. chopped mint
1 egg white
2 garlic cloves, chopped

2 tsp. harissa
1 tsp. pepper
1 tsp. salt
¼ cup olive oil
1 tsp. cumin
1 tsp. coriander

Yogurt:

¼ cup chopped mint
¼ cup sour cream
½ cup yogurt

2 tbsp. buttermilk
1 garlic clove, minced
¼ tsp. salt

Directions:

1. Preheat the air fryer to 390 degrees F.
2. Combine all of the meatball ingredients in a large bowl.
3. Wet your hands and make meatballs out of the mixture.
4. Cook the meatballs for 8 minutes. You will have to work in two batches.
5. Meanwhile, combine all of the yogurt ingredients in another bowl.
6. Serve the meatballs topped with yogurt.

Melty and Gooey Chicken Sandwich

(Prep + Cook Time: 12 minutes / Serving: 1)

Nutritional info per serving:

Calories 650, Proteins 32g, Carbohydrates 34.4g, Fats 34.8g

Ingredients:

¼ cup cooked and shredded chicken breasts (preferably leftovers)
¼ cup shredded cabbage
2 mozzarella slices
¼ cup grated cheddar cheese
½ tsp. balsamic vinegar
1 tsp. olive oil
Salt and pepper, to taste
2 tsp. butter
2 slices of bread
¼ tsp. smoked paprika
1 tsp. mayonnaise

Directions:

1. Spread the butter on the outside of the bread.
2. Place the chicken on top of the inside of 1 slice of bread.
3. Top with mayonnaise and smoked paprika.
4. Arrange the mozzarella slices over.
5. Combine the cabbage with olive oil and balsamic vinegar and season with some salt and pepper in a bowl.
6. Top the mozzarella with the cabbage mixture.
7. Arrange the cheddar on top of the cabbage.
8. Top with the other bread slice.
9. Soak 2 toothpicks in water to avoid burning them.
10. Secure the sandwich with the toothpicks.
11. Place in the air fryer and cook for 7 minutes.
12. Cut the sandwich in half.

Mock Stir Fry

(Prep + Cook Time: 25 minutes / Servings: 4)

Nutritional info per serving:

Calories 277, Carbohydrates 15.6 g, Fat 4.4 g, Protein 43.1 g

Ingredients:

4 boneless and skinless chicken breasts cut into cubes
2 carrots, sliced
1 red bell pepper, cut into strips
1 yellow bell pepper, cut into strips
1 cup snow peas
15 oz. broccoli florets
1 scallion, sliced

Sauce:

3 tbsp. soy sauce
2 tbsp. oyster sauce
1 tbsp. brown sugar
1 tsp. sesame oil
1 tsp. cornstarch
1 tsp. sriracha
2 garlic cloves, minced
1 tbsp. grated ginger
1 tbsp. rice wine vinegar

Directions:

1. Preheat the air fryer to 370 degrees F.
2. Place the chicken, bell peppers, and carrot, in a bowl.
3. In a small bowl, combine the sauce ingredients.
4. Coat the chicken mixture with the sauce.
5. Place on a lined baking sheet and cook for 5 minutes.
6. Add snow peas and broccoli and cook for additional 8 to10 minutes.
7. Serve garnished with scallion.

Prosciutto and Mozzarella Bruschetta

(Prep + Cook Time: 7 minutes / Serving: 1)

Nutritional info per serving:

Calories 674.6, Carbohydrates 41.6 g, Fat 38.8 g, Protein 38.4 g

Ingredients:

½ cup finely chopped tomatoes
3 oz. chopped mozzarella
3 prosciutto slices, chopped

1 tbsp. olive oil
1 tsp. dried basil
6 small slices of French bread

Directions:

1. Preheat the air fryer to 350 degrees F. Place the bread slices and toast for about 3 minutes. Top the bread with tomatoes, prosciutto and mozzarella.
2. Sprinkle the basil over the mozzarella. Drizzle with olive oil.
3. Return to the air fryer and cook for 1 more minute, enough to become melty and warm.

Potato and Bacon Salad

(Prep + Cook Time: 10 minutesServings: 10)

Nutritional info per serving:

Calories 306.5, Carbohydrates 33.9 g, Fat 14.9 g, Protein 10 g

Ingredients:

4 lb. boiled and cubed potatoes
15 bacon slices, chopped
2 cups shredded cheddar cheese

15 oz. sour cream
2 tbsp. mayonnaise
1 tsp. dried herbs, any

Directions:

1. Preheat the air fryer to 350 degrees F. Combine the potatoes, bacon, salt, pepper, and herbs, in a large bowl. Transfer to a baking dish.
2. Cook for about 7 minutes. Stir in sour cream and mayonnaise.

Side Dishes and Snacks

Air Fried Potatoes Au Gratin

(Prep + Cook Time: 45 minutes / Servings: 6)

Nutritional info per serving:

Calories 289, Carbohydrates 50.4 g, Fat 6.1 g, Protein 9.2 g

Ingredients:

5 large potatoes
½ cup sour cream
½ cup grated cheese
½ cup milk
½ tsp. nutmeg
½ tsp. black pepper
½ tsp. salt

Directions:

1. Preheat the air fryer to 390 degrees F.
2. Peel and slice the potatoes.
3. In a bowl, combine the sour cream, milk, pepper, salt and nutmeg.
4. Place the potato slices in the bowl with the milk mixture and stir to coat them well.
5. Transfer the whole mixture to a baking dish.
6. Cook for 25 minutes.
7. Sprinkle the grated cheese on top.
8. Cook for 10 more minutes.

Cheesy Prosciutto Croquettes

(Prep + Cook Time: 50 minutes / Servings: 6)

Nutritional info per serving:

Calories 314, Carbohydrates 11.2 g, Fat 21.9 g, Protein 12.4 g

Ingredients:

1 lb. cheddar cheese
12 slices of prosciutto
1 cup flour

2 eggs, beaten
4 tbsp. olive oil
1 cup breadcrumbs

Directions:

1. Cut the cheese into 6 equal pieces. Wrap each piece of cheese with 2 prosciutto slices. Place them in the freezer just enough to set. I left mine for about 5 minutes. Note that they mustn't be frozen.
2. Meanwhile, Preheat the air fryer to 390 degrees F.
3. Dip the croquettes into the flour first then the egg, and then coat them with the breadcrumbs.
4. Place the olive oil in the basket of the air fryer and cook the croquettes for 8 minutes, or until golden.

Air Fried Pickles

(Prep + Cook Time: 15 minutes / Servings: 2)

Nutritional info per serving:

Calories 309, Carbohydrates 42.8 g, Fat 11.3 g, Protein 10.4 g

Ingredients:

8 medium pickles
1 egg, beaten
½ cup breadcrumbs

1 tsp. paprika
4 tbsp. flour
1 tbsp. olive oil

Directions:

1. Preheat the air fryer to 350 degrees F.
2. Cut the pickles lengthwise and pat them dry.
3. Combine the flour, paprika and salt, in a small bowl.
4. In another bowl, combine the breadcrumbs and olive oil.
5. Dredge in the flour first, dip them in the beaten egg, and then coat them with the breadcrumbs.
6. Arrange on a lined baking sheet and place in the air fryer.
7. Cook for 10 minutes, or to your liking.
8. Serve with favorite dipping sauce and enjoy.

Sweet Mascarpone Figs

(Prep + Cook Time: 10 minutes / Servings: 4)

Nutritional info per serving:

Calories 267, Carbohydrates 28.8 g, Fat 16.7 g, Protein 1.7 g

Ingredients:

8 figs
6 oz. mascarpone cheese
1 tsp. rose water

1 oz. butter
3 tbsp. honey
2 tbsp. toasted almond slices

Directions:

1. Preheat the air fryer to 350 degrees F.
2. Open the figs by cutting a cross on top and gently squeezing them.
3. Divide the honey between the figs.
4. Place them on a lined baking sheet. Cook for 5 minutes.
5. Combine the mascarpone with the rose water.
6. Place a dollop of the mascarpone onto each fig. Top with toasted almonds.
7. Enjoy.

Grilled Lime Corn

(Prep + Cook Time: 20 minutes / Servings: 2)

Nutritional info per serving:

Calories 246.8, Carbohydrates 21.5 g, Fat 13.3 g, Protein 11.4 g

Ingredients:

2 ears of corn
Juice of 2 small limes
2 tsp. paprika

4 oz. feta cheese
Olive oil

Directions:

1. Preheat the air fryer to 370 degrees.
2. Peel the corn and remove the silk.
3. Place the feta cheese in the freezer.
4. Drizzle some olive oil into the air fryer.
5. Place the corn and cook for 15 minutes.
6. Squeeze the juice of 1 lime on top of each ear of corn.
7. Take the cheese out of the freezer and grate onto corn.

Mozzarella Cheese Sticks

(Prep + Cook Time: 40 minutes / Servings: 2)

Nutritional info per serving:

Calories 274.3, Carbohydrates 22.2 g, Fat 11.7 g, Protein 19.4 g

Ingredients:

8 oz. mozzarella cheese
1 tsp. garlic powder
1 egg

1 cup breadcrumbs
½ tsp. salt
Olive oil

Directions:

1. Cut the mozzarella into 6 strips. Whisk the egg along with the salt and garlic powder.
2. Dip the mozzarella into the egg mixture first, and then into the breadcrumbs.
3. Arrange them on a platter and place in the freezer for about 20 to 30 minutes.
4. Preheat the air fryer to 370 degrees. Drizzle some olive oil into the air fryer.
5. Arrange the mozzarella sticks in the air fryer and cook for about 5 minutes.
6. Make sure to turn them over at least 2 times, to ensure that they will be evenly golden on all sides.

Veggie Ham Rolls with Cashew Nuts

(Prep + Cook Time: 15 minutes / Servings: 4)

Nutritional info per serving:

Calories 214, Carbohydrates 23 g, Fat 8 g, Protein 11 g

Ingredients:

8 rice leaves
4 carrots
4 slices ham
2 oz. cashew nuts, finely chopped
1 zucchini
1 clove garlic
1 tbsp. olive oil
1 tbsp. ginger powder
1/4 cup basil leaves, finely chopped
salt and pepper

Directions:

1. In a cooking pan, pour olive oil and add the zucchini, carrots, garlic, ginger and salt. Cook on low heat for 10 minutes.
2. Add the basil and cashew nuts, and keep stirring.
3. Soak the rice leaves in warm water. Then fold one side above the filling and roll in.
4. Put the rolls in the preheated Air Fryer and cook them for 5 minutes at 300° F.

Cauliflower Buffalo

(Prep + Cook Time: 20 minutes / Servings: 4)

Nutritional info per serving:

Calories 239.2, Carbohydrates 28 g, Fat 13.5 g, Protein 6.1 g

Ingredients:

4 cups cauliflower florets
¼ cup butter, melted
¼ cup buffalo sauce
1 cup breadcrumbs

Directions:

1. Whisk the buffalo sauce along with the butter.
2. In a shallow bowl, combine the breadcrumb with the sea salt.
3. Dip each cauliflower floret into the buffalo mixture first, and then coat in breadcrumbs.
4. Drop the prepared florets into the air fryer.
5. Set the temperature to 350 degrees F and set the timer for 15 minutes.
6. Shake the florets a couple of time.
7. Serve with your favorite dipping or as a side dish.

Air Fried Bananas

(Prep + Cook Time: 6 minutes / Servings: 6)

Nutritional info per serving:

Calories 219.2, Carbohydrates 48.5 g, Fat 5.5 g, Protein 4.1 g

Ingredients:

6 bananas
4 large eggs, beaten
1 cup breadcrumbs
1 cup bread flour
1 cup oil

Directions:

1. Peel the bananas and cut them into pieces of less than 1-inch each.
2. Mix the beaten eggs with the bread flour and the oil.
3. Dredge the banana first into the flour, then dip them in the beaten eggs, then in the breadcrumbs.
4. Line the banana pieces in the Air Fryer and fry them for 10 minutes at 350° F.

Pigs in Blankets

(Prep + Cook Time: 15 minutes / Servings: 4)

Nutritional info per serving:

Calories 238, Carbohydrates 25.4 g, Fat 9.4 g, Protein 8.4 g

Ingredients:

8 oz. crescent rolls

12 oz. cocktail hot dogs

Directions:

1. Preheat the air fryer to 330 degrees F.
2. On a clean and dry surface, cut the dough into 1-inch rectangles.
3. Roll each strip around each of the hot dogs.
4. Line a baking sheet with parchment paper.
5. Arrange the pigs in blanket on the lined sheet.
6. Cook for 6 minutes.
7. Raise the temperature to 390 degrees F, and cook for additional 3 minutes.
8. Enjoy.

Chorizo Empanadas

(Prep + Cook Time: 15 minutes / Servings: 3)

Nutritional info per serving:

Calories 368, Carbohydrates 21 g, Fat 31 g, Protein 26.9 g

Ingredients:

9 oz. pizza dough
6 oz. chorizo, cubed
2 tbsp. of parsley

1 shallot, finely chopped
½ red bell pepper, cubed

Directions:

1. In a skillet, mix the chorizo, the bell pepper and the shallot and fry on low heat for around 5 minutes. Switch off the heat and add the parsley.
2. Set the mixture aside and preheat the Air Fryer to 350° F.
3. Using a pin, roll the dough to half inch of thickness.
4. With a water glass or steel rings, cut the dough in 22-23 rounds of 2 inches each. Scoop 1 spoon of the chorizo mixture o on each of the rounds.
5. Press all the edges between the thumb and the index finger to create a scallop shape. Place the empanadas in the Air Fryer and fry for 8 minutes or until brown.

Air Fried Potatoes with Eggs and Cheese

(Prep + Cook Time: 24 minutes / Servings: 3)

Nutritional info per serving:

Calories 226, Carbohydrates 25.1 g, Fat 9.1 g, Protein 8.7 g

Ingredients:

3 potatoes, sliced
2 eggs, beaten
2 oz. cheddar cheese

1 tbsp. all-purpose flour
100 ml coconut cream

Directions:

1. Remove the skin of the thin sliced potatoes and place them in the Air Fryer. Cook for 12 minutes at 350° F.
2. To prepare the sauce, mix the two beaten eggs, the coconut cream and the flour until all the cream mixture thickens.
3. Remove the potatoes from the Air Fryer.
4. Line them in the ramekin and top with the cream mixture and the cheese.
5. Cover the potatoes and cook for 12 more minutes.

Potato Chips Creamy Dip

(Prep + Cook Time: 25 minutes / Servings: 3)

Nutritional info per serving:

Calories 271, Carbohydrates 29.2 g, Fat 11.8 g, Protein 12.2 g

Ingredients:

3 large potatoes
1 cup sour cream
2 scallions, white part minced

3 tbsp. olive oil.
½ tsp. lemon juice
salt and black pepper

Directions:

1. Preheat the Air Fryer to 350° F.
2. Slice the potatoes into thin slices. Do not peel them.
3. Soak them in water for 10 minutes, then dry them and spray with oil.
4. Fry the potato slices in two separate batches for 15 minutes.
5. Season with salt and pepper.
6. To prepare the dip, mix the sour cream, olive oil, the scallions, the lemon juice, salt and pepper.

Pumpkin Ham Fritters

(Prep + Cook Time: 10 minutes / Servings: 4)

Nutritional info per serving:

Calories 211, Carbohydrates 35.2 g, Fat 16.5 g, Protein 10.2 g

Ingredients:

1 oz. ham, chopped
1 cup dry pancake mix
1 egg
2 tbsp. canned pure pumpkin
1 oz. cheddar, shredded

½ tsp. chili powder
3 tbsp. of flour.
1 oz. beer
2 tbsp. scallions, chopped

Directions:

1. Preheat the Air Fryer to 370° F.
2. In a bowl, mix the pancake mix and the chili powder.
3. Add the egg and the canned pure pumpkin, the beer, the shredded cheddar, the ham and the scallions. Roll the mixture in 3 tbsp. of flour.
4. Range the balls into the basket and cook for 8 minutes.
5. Drain on paper towel before serving.

Parmesan and Garlic French Fries

(Prep + Cook Time: 30 minutes / Servings: 5)

Nutritional info per serving:

Calories 174.2, Carbohydrates 23.7 g, Fat 7.3 g, Protein 4 g

Ingredients:

1 ½ lb. potatoes
3 tbsp. Parmesan cheese
1 tbsp. minced garlic

2 tbsp. olive oil
Salt and pepper, to taste

Directions:

1. Preheat the air fryer to 390 degrees.
2. Peel and slice the potatoes in large and slim slices.
3. Place the potatoes in a large bowl.
4. Add olive oil, garlic, and season with some salt and pepper. Stir to combine them well.
5. Place the potatoes in the basket of the air fryer and sprinkle the Parmesan cheese over them.
6. Bake for about 20 minutes.
7. Enjoy.

Salty and Vinegary Zucchini Chips

(Prep + Cook Time: 20 minutes / Servings: 4)

Nutritional info per serving:

Calories 92, Carbohydrates 8.1 g, Fat 6.8 g, Protein 1.2 g

Ingredients:

3 medium zucchini
2 tsp. sea salt
2 tbsp. olive oil
2 tbsp. balsamic vinegar

Directions:

1. Preheat the air fryer to 390 degrees.
2. Wash the zucchini well and trim off the ends.
3. Pat them dry and slice them very thinly.
4. Place the zucchini in a large bowl.
5. Add the remaining ingredients. Using your hands, mix the zucchini to coat them well.
6. Place them in the basket of the air fryer and cook for 15 minutes.
7. Enjoy.

Poultry Recipes

Buffalo Chicken

(Prep + Cook Time: 25 minutes / Servings: 4)

Nutritional info per serving:

Calories 321, Carbohydrates 25.5 g, Fat 8.8 g, Protein 34.5 g

Ingredients:

1 cup breadcrumbs
½ cup yogurt
1 lb. chicken breasts cut into strips
1 tbsp. ground cayenne

1 tbsp. hot sauce
2 beaten eggs
1 tbsp. sweet paprika
1 tbsp. garlic powder

Directions:

1. Preheat the air fryer to 390 degrees F. Whisk the eggs along with the hot sauce and yogurt. In a shallow bowl, combine the breadcrumbs, paprika, pepper, and garlic powder. Line a baking dish with parchment paper.
2. Dip the chicken in the egg/yogurt mixture first, and then coat with breadcrumbs. Arrange on the sheet and bake in the air fryer for 8 minutes.
3. Flip the chicken over and bake for 8 more minutes on the other side.

Pineapple Chicken

(Prep + Cook Time: 20 minutes / Servings: 2)

Nutritional info per serving:

Calories 355, Carbohydrates 35 g, Fat 11 g, Protein 32 g

Ingredients:

2 large chicken breasts, cubed
2 green bell peppers, sliced

½ onion, sliced
1 can drained pineapple chunks
½ cup barbecue sauce
6 skewers

Directions:

1. Preheat the Air Fryer to 370° F.
2. Thread the green bell peppers, the chicken, the onions and the pineapple chunks on the skewers.
3. Brush with barbecue sauce and fry for 20 minutes.

Crunchy Chicken Fingers

(Prep + Cook Time: 8 minutes / Servings: 2)

Nutritional info per serving:

Calories 253, Carbohydrates 31 g, Fat 18 g, Protein 28 g

Ingredients:

2 medium-sized chicken breasts, cut in stripes
3 tbsp. parmesan cheese
¼ tsp of fresh chives, chopped
⅓ cup breadcrumbs
1 egg white
2 tsp plum sauce, optional
½ tsp. fresh thyme, chopped
½ tsp. black pepper
1 tsp. of water

Directions:

1. Preheat the Air Fryer to 360° F.
2. Mix the chives, parmesan, thyme, pepper and breadcrumbs.
3. In another bowl, whisk the egg white and and mix with the water.
4. Dip the chicken strips into egg mixture and the bread crumb mixture.
5. Place the strips in the air fryer basket and cook for 10 minutes.
6. Serve with plum sauce.

Air Fried Chicken with Black Beans

(Prep + Cook Time: 18 minutes / Servings: 4)

Nutritional info per serving:

Calories 368, Carbohydrates 56 g, Fat 8 g, Protein 45 g

Ingredients:

4 boneless and skinless chicken breasts, in pieces of 1-inch
1 can sweet corn
1 can rinsed and drained black beans
1 cup red and green peppers, stripes, cooked
1 tbsp. vegetable oil
2 tsp. chili powder

Directions:

1. Coat the chicken with salt, black pepper and a sprinkle of oil.
2. Cook it for 15 minutes at 380° F.
3. Meanwhile, in a deep skillet, pour 1 tbsp. of oil and stir in the chili powder, the corn and the beans.
4. Add a little bit of hot water and keep stirring for 3 more minutes.
5. Transfer the corn, the beans and the chicken to a serving platter.
6. Enjoy.

Quick and Crispy Chicken

(Prep + Cook Time: 15 minutes / Servings: 4)

Nutritional info per serving:

Calories 218, Carbohydrates 25.3 g, Fat 8.5 g, Protein 29.5 g

Ingredients:

8 chicken tenderloins
2 tbsp. butter
2 oz. breadcrumbs
1 large egg, whisked

Directions:

1. Preheat the air fryer to 380° F. Combine the butter and the breadcrumbs.
2. Keep mixing and stirring until the mixture gets crumbly.
3. Dip the chicken in the egg wash. Then dip the chicken in the crumbs mix.
4. Making sure it is evenly and fully covered. Cook for 10 minutes.
5. Serve the dish and enjoy its crispy taste!

Chicken with Rice

(Prep + Cook Time: 40 minutes / Servings: 4)

Nutritional info per serving:

Calories 418, Carbohydrates 76 g, Fat 21 g, Protein 38 g

Ingredients:

4 chicken legs
1 cup rice
2 cups water
2 tomatoes, cubed
3 tbsp. of butter
1 tbsp. tomato paste
salt and black pepper
1 onion
3 minced cloves of garlic

Directions:

1. Rub the chicken legs with butter.
2. Sprinkle with salt and pepper and fry it in a preheated Air Fryer for 30 minutes at 380° F.
3. Then add the small onion and a little bit of oil, and keep stirring.
4. Add the tomatoes, the tomato paste, and the garlic and cook for 5 more minutes.
5. Meanwhile, in a pan boil the rice in 2 cups of water for around 20 minutes.
6. In a baking tray, place the rice and top it with the air fried chicken and place in the Air Fryer for 5 minutes.

Mustard and Maple Turkey Breast

(Prep + Cook Time: 1 hour / Servings: 6)

Nutritional info per serving:

Calories 529.6, Carbohydrates 77 g, Fat 20 g, Protein 13 g

Ingredients:

5 lb. of whole turkey breast
¼ cup maple syrup
2 tbsp. Dijon mustard
½ tsp. smoked paprika
1 tsp. thyme

2 tsp. olive oil
½ tsp. sage
½ tsp. salt and black pepper
1 tbsp. butter, melted

Directions:

1. Preheat the air fryer to 350 degrees F.
2. Brush the turkey with the olive oil.
3. Combine all the herbs and seasoning in a small bowl, and rub the turkey with the mixture.
4. Air fry the turkey for about 25 minutes.
5. Flip the turkey on its side and continue cooking for additional 12 minutes.
6. Now, turn on the opposite side, and again, cook for additional 12 minutes.
7. Meanwhile, whisk the butter, maple and mustard together in a small bowl.
8. When done, brush the glaze all over the turkey.
9. Return to the air fryer and cook for 5 more minutes.
10. Enjoy.

Air Fried Chicken with Honey and Lemon

(Prep + Cook Time: 100 minutes / Servings: 6)

Nutritional info per serving:

Calories 342, Carbohydrates 68 g, Fat 28 g, Protein 33 g

Ingredients:

The Stuffing:

1 whole chicken, 3 lb.
2 red and peeled onions
2 tbsp. of olive oil
2 apricots
1 yellow zucchini
1 apple
2 cloves of finely chopped garlic
fresh chopped thyme
salt and pepper

The Marinade:

5 oz. of honey
the juice from 1 large lemon
2 tbsp. of olive oil
salt and pepper

Directions:

1. For the stuffing, chop all the ingredients into tiny pieces.
2. Transfer the ingredients to a large bowl and add the olive oil.
3. Season with salt and black pepper.
4. Fill the cavity of the chicken with the stuffing, without packing it tightly.
5. Place the chicken in the Air Fryer and cook for 35 minutes at 340° F.
6. Meanwhile, warm the honey and the lemon juice in a large pan and season with salt and pepper. Reduce the temperature of the Air Fryer to 320° F.
7. Brush the chicken with some of the honey-lemon marinade and return it back to the Air Fryer. Cook for another 65-70 minutes.
8. Make sure to brush the chicken every 20-25 minutes with the marinade.
9. Garnish with chopped parsley. Serve with potatoes, rice or salad.

Chicken Breasts with Tarragon

(Prep + Cook Time: 15 minutes / Servings: 3)

Nutritional info per serving:

Calories 329, Carbohydrates 56 g, Fat 23 g, Protein 23 g

Ingredients:

1 boneless and skinless chicken breast
½ tbsp. butter
¼ tsp kosher salt
¼ cup dried tarragon
¼ tsp black and fresh ground pepper

Directions:

1. Preheat the Air Fryer to 380° F.
2. Place each chicken breast on a 12x12 inches foil wrap.
3. Top the chicken with tarragon and butter. Salt and pepper to taste.
4. Wrap the foil around the chicken breast in a loose way to create a flow of air.
5. Cook the in the Air Fryer for 15 minutes.
6. Carefully unwrap the chicken and serve.

Cajun Chicken Tenders

(Prep + Cook Time: 25 minutes / Servings: 4)

Nutritional info per serving:

Calories 493, Carbohydrates 36.5 g, Fat 11 g, Protein 57.5 g

Ingredients:

3 lb. chicken breast cut into slices
3 eggs
2 ¼ cup flour, divided
1 tbsp. olive oil
½ tbsp. plus
½ tsp. garlic powder, divided
3 tsp. Cajun seasoning, divided
¼ cup milk

Directions:

1. Season the chicken with salt, pepper, ½ tsp. garlic powder and 2 tsp. Cajun seasoning.
2. Combine 2 cups flour, the rest of the Cajun seasoning and the rest of the garlic powder, in a bowl.
3. In another bowl, whisk the eggs, milk, olive oil, and quarter cup flour.
4. Preheat the air fryer to 370 degrees F. Line a baking sheet with parchment paper. Dip the chicken into the egg mixture first, and then into the flour mixture.
5. Arrange on the sheet. If there isn't enough room, work in two batches.
6. Bake for about 12 to 15 minutes.

Chicken with Cashew Nuts

(Prep + Cook Time: 30 minutes / Servings: 4)

Nutritional info per serving:

Calories 425, Carbohydrates 25 g, Fat 35 g, Protein 53 g

Ingredients:

1 lb. chicken cubes
2 tbsp. soya sauce
1 tbsp. corn flour
2 ½ onion cubes
1 carrot, chopped

⅓ cup cashew nuts, fried
1 capsicum, cut
2 tbsp. garlic, crushed
salt and white pepper

Directions:

1. Marinate the chicken cubes with ½ tsp of white pepper, ½ tsp of salt, 2 tbsp. of soya sauce, and add 1 tbsp. of corn flour. Set aside for 25 minutes.
2. Preheat the Air Fryer to 380° F and transfer the marinated chicken.
3. Add the garlic, the onion, the capsicum, and the carrot. Fry for 5-6 minutes.
4. Roll it in the cashew nuts before serving.

Crunchy Coconut Chicken

(Prep + Cook Time: 22 minutes / Servings: 4)

Nutritional info per serving:

Calories 780, Carbohydrates 21.6 g, Fat 47 g, Protein 66 g

Ingredients:

3 ½ cups coconut flakes
4 chicken breasts cut into strips
½ cup cornstarch
3 eggs, beaten

Directions:

1. Preheat the air fryer to 350 degrees F.
2. Mix salt, pepper, and cornstarch in a small bowl.
3. Line a baking sheet with parchment paper.
4. Dip the chicken first in the cornstarch, then into the eggs, and finally, coat it with coconut flakes.
5. Arrange on the sheet and cook for about 8 minutes.
6. Flip the chicken over and cook for 8 more minutes.

Air Fried Southern Drumsticks

(Prep + Cook Time: 50 minutes / Servings: 4)

Nutritional info per serving:

Calories 197, Carbohydrates 5.2, Fat 6 g, Protein 29.2 g

Ingredients:

8 chicken drumsticks
2 tbsp. oregano
2 tbsp. thyme
2 oz. oats
¼ cup milk
¼ steamed cauliflower florets
1 egg
1 tsp. ground cayenne

Directions:

1. Preheat the air fryer to 350 degrees F. Season the drumsticks with salt and pepper. Rub them with the milk.
2. Place all of the other ingredients, except the egg, in a food processor. Process until really smooth.
3. Dip each drumstick in the egg first, and then in the oat mixture.
4. Arrange half of them on a baking mat inside the air fryer.
5. Cook for 20 minutes. Repeat with the other batch.

Fried Chicken Legs

(Prep + Cook Time: 50 minutes / Servings: 5)

Nutritional info per serving:

Calories 288, Carbohydrates 15g, Fat 11 g, Protein 35 g

Ingredients:

5 quarters chicken legs
2 lemons, halved
5 tsp. of garlic powder
5 tsp. of dried basil
5 tbsp. of oregano, dried
⅓ cup of olive oil
salt and black pepper

Directions:

1. Set the Air Fryer to 350° F.
2. Place the chicken in a large deep bowl.
3. Brush the chicken legs with a tablespoon of olive oil.
4. Sprinkle with the lemon juice and arrange it in the Air Fryer.
5. In a another bowl, combine the basil, the oregano, the garlic powder, salt and pepper.
6. Sprinkle the seasoning mixture on the chicken.
7. Cook in the preheated Air Fryer for 50 minutes.

Turkey Cordon Bleu

(Prep + Cook Time: 35 minutes / Servings: 4)

Nutritional info per serving:

Calories 316, Carbohydrates 17g, Fat 9 g, Protein 37 g

Ingredients:

2 turkey breasts	1 tsp. garlic powder
1 ham slice	1 tsp. thyme
1 slice cheddar cheese	1 tsp. tarragon
2 oz. breadcrumbs	1 egg, beaten
1 tbsp. cream cheese	Salt and pepper, to taste

Directions:

1. Preheat the air fryer to 350 degrees F.
2. Cut the turkey in the middle, that way so you can add ingredients in the center.
3. Season the turkey with salt, pepper, thyme and tarragon.
4. Combine the cream cheese and garlic powder in a small bowl.
5. Spread the mixture on the inside of the breasts.
6. Place half a cheddar slice and half a ham slice in the center of each breast.
7. Dip the cordon bleu in egg first, and then sprinkle with breadcrumbs.
8. Cook on a baking mat for 30 minutes.

Beef, Pork and Lamb Recipes

Roast Beef

(Prep + Cook Time: 60 minutes / Servings: 8)

Nutritional info per serving:

Calories 366, Carbohydrates 7 g, Fat 31 g, Protein 18 g

Ingredients:

2 lb. beef loin
½ tsp. black pepper, salt
1 tsp. thyme
1 tsp. rosemary

½ tsp. oregano
½ tsp. garlic powder
1 tsp. onion powder
1 tbsp. olive oil

Directions:

1. Preheat the air fryer to 330 degrees F. In a small bowl, combine the olive oil and seasonings. Rub the mixture into the beef. Place the beef in the basket of the air fryer and cook for 30 minutes.
2. Turn the roast over and cook for 20 to 30 more minutes.

Healthier Burgers

(Prep + Cook Time: 20 minutes / Servings: 4)

Nutritional info per serving:

Calories 366, Carbohydrates 6 g, Fat 31 g, Protein 18 g

Ingredients:

1 lb. ground beef
½ tsp. onion powder
½ tsp. oregano
1 tbsp. Worcestershire sauce

½ tsp. garlic powder
1 tsp. parsley
1 tsp. Maggi seasoning sauce
1 tsp. olive oil

Directions:

1. Preheat the air fryer to 350 degrees F. Combine all of the sauces and seasonings, except oil, in a small bowl.
2. Place the beef in a bowl and stir in the seasonings. Mix until the mixture is very well incorporated.
3. Divide the meat mixture into four equal pieces and form patties.
4. Place the olive oil in the air fryer.
5. Arrange the 4 burgers in the fryer and cook for 10 to 15 minutes.

Meatballs in Tomato Sauce

(Prep + Cook Time: 20 minutes / Servings: 4)

Nutritional info per serving:

Calories 386, Carbohydrates 26 g, Fat 21 g, Protein 35 g

Ingredients:

½ lb. ground beef
1 medium onion
1 egg
4 tbsp. breadcrumbs

1 tbsp. fresh parsley, chopped
½ tbsp. thyme leaves, chopped
10 oz. of tomato sauce
salt and pepper

Directions

1. Place all ingredients into a bowl and mix very well.
2. Shape the mixture into 10 to 12 balls.
3. Preheat the Air Fryer to 380° F.
4. Place the meatballs in the air fryer basket, and fry them for 10 minutes.
5. Remove the meatballs and place them in an oven plate.
6. Add in the tomato sauce and place them back in the Air Fryer.
7. Lower the temperature to 300° F.
8. Cook for 6 more minutes.

Liver Soufflé

(Prep + Cook Time: 40 minutes / Servings: 4)

Nutritional info per serving:

Calories 216, Carbohydrates 25 g, Fat 17 g, Protein 42 g

Ingredients:

½ lb. of liver
3 eggs

3 oz. buns
1 cup warm milk

Directions:

1. Cut the liver in slices and put it in the fridge for 15 minutes.
2. Divide the buns into pieces and soak them in milk for 10 minutes.
3. Put the liver in a blender, and add the yolks, the bread mixture and the spices.
4. Grind the components and stuff in the ramekins.
5. Line the ramekins in the Air Fryer's basket and cook for 20 minutes at 350° F.

Air Fried Beef Empanada

(Prep + Cook Time: 25 minutes / Servings: 4)

Nutritional info per serving:

Calories 495, Carbohydrates 17 g, Fat 36 g, Protein 23 g

Ingredients:

1 lb. ground beef
½ onion, diced
1 garlic clove, minced
¼ cup tomato salsa
4 empanada shells

1 egg yolk
2 tsp. milk
½ tsp. cumin
Salt and pepper, to taste
½ tbsp. olive oil

Directions:

1. Place the olive oil in the air fryer and preheat it to 350 degrees F. Meanwhile, combine the beef, onion, cumin, and garlic, in a bowl. Season with some salt and pepper.
2. Place the beef in the air fryer and cook for about 7 minutes. Stir in the tomato salsa and set aside.
3. In a small bowl, combine the milk and yolk. Place the empanada shells on a dry and clean surface.
4. Divide the beef mixture between the shells. Fold the shells and seal the ends with a fork. Brush with the egg wash.
5. Place on a lined baking sheet and bake at 350 degrees F for about 10 minutes.

Liver Muffins with Eggs

(Prep + Cook Time: 25 minutes / Servings: 2)

Nutritional info per serving:

Calories 345, Carbohydrates 45 g, Fat 26 g, Protein 43 g

Ingredients:

1 lb. beef liver, sliced
2 large eggs
1 tbsp. of butter
½ tbsp. of black truffle oil
1 tbsp. of cream
salt and black pepper

Directions:

1. Preheat the Air Fryer to 320° F. Cut the liver into thin slices and put it in the fridge for 10 minutes. Separate the whites from the yolks and put each yolk in a cup.
2. In another bowl, add the cream, truffle oil, salt and pepper and mix with a fork. Arrange half of the mixture in a small ramekin.
3. Pour the white of the egg and divide it equally between ramekins.
4. Top with the egg yolks. Surround each yolk with liver.
5. Cook for 15 minutes and serve cool.

The Simples and Yummiest Rib Eye Steak

(Prep + Cook Time: 20 minutes / Servings: 6)

Nutritional info per serving:

Calories 219, Carbohydrates 10 g, Fat 8 g, Protein 34 g

Ingredients:

2 lb. rib eye steak
1 tbsp. steak rub
1 tbsp. olive oil

Directions:

1. Preheat the air fryer to 400 degrees F.
2. Combine the steak rub and olive oil.
3. Rub the steak with the seasoning.
4. Place in the air fryer and cook for about 10 minutes.
5. Flip the steak over and cook for 7 more minutes.
6. Enjoy.

Panko Beef Schnitzel

(Prep + Cook Time: 22 minutes / Servings: 1)

Nutritional info per serving:

Calories 686, Carbohydrates 41g, Fat 39.5 g, Protein 40 g

Ingredients:

2 tbsp. olive oil
1 thin beef cutlet
1 egg, beaten
2 oz. breadcrumbs
1 tsp. paprika
¼ tsp. garlic powder
Salt and pepper, to taste

Directions:

1. Preheat the air fryer to 350 degrees F.
2. Combine all of the olive oil, breadcrumbs, paprika, garlic powder and salt and.
3. Dip the beef in with the egg first, and then coat it with the breadcrumb mixture completely.
4. Line a baking dish with parchment paper and place the breaded meat on it.
5. Cook for about 12 minutes.
6. Serve as desired.
7. Enjoy.

Beef Bulgogi

(Prep + Cook Time: 3 hours 15 minutes / Servings: 1)

Nutritional info per serving:

Calories 599, Carbohydrates 10 g, Fat 24 g, Protein 33 g

Ingredients:

6 oz. beef
½ cup sliced mushrooms
2 tbsp. bulgogi marinade
1 tbsp. diced onion

Directions:

1. Cut the beef into small pieces and place it in a bowl.
2. Add the bulgogi and mix to coat the beef completely.
3. Cover the bowl and place in the fridge for about 3 hours to marinate.
4. Preheat the air fryer to 350 degrees F. Transfer the beef to a baking dish.
5. Stir in the mushroom and onion. Cook for about 10 minutes.
6. Serve with some roasted potatoes and green salad.

The Ultimate Beef Chili

(Prep + Cook Time: 50 minutes / Servings: 6)

Nutritional info per serving:

Calories 485, Carbohydrates 38 g, Fat 28 g, Protein 39 g

Ingredients:

- 1 lb. ground beef
- ½ tbsp. chili powder
- 1 tsp. salt
- 1 can (8 oz.) cannellini beans
- 1 tsp. chopped cilantro
- 1 tbsp. olive oil
- ½ tsp. parsley
- ½ cup chopped celery
- 1 onion, chopped
- 2 garlic cloves, minced
- 1 ½ cup vegetable broth
- ¼ tsp. pepper
- 1 can diced tomatoes
- ½ cup finely chopped bell pepper

Directions:

1. Preheat the air fryer to 350 degrees F.
2. Place the oil, garlic, onion, bell pepper, and celery, in an ovenproof bowl.
3. Place the bowl in the air fryer and cook for 5 minutes.
4. Add the beef and cook for 6 more minutes.
5. Stir in broth, tomatoes, chili, parsley, and coriander.
6. Let cook for 20 minutes.
7. Stir in beans, salt, and pepper.
8. Cook for 10 more minutes.
9. Sprinkle with cilantro and enjoy.
10. Enjoy.

Vegetarian Recipes

Nutty Pumpkin with Blue Cheese

(Prep + Cook Time: 30 minutes / Servings: 1)

Nutritional info per serving:

Calories 495, Carbohydrates 29 g, Fat 27 g, Protein 9 g

Ingredients:

½ small pumpkin
2 oz. blue cheese, cubed
2 tbsp. pine nuts
1 tbsp. olive oil

½ cup baby spinach, packed
1 spring onion, sliced
1 radish, thinly sliced
1 tsp. vinegar

Directions:

1. Preheat the air fryer to 330 degrees F.
2. Place the pine nuts in a baking dish and toast them for 5 minutes.
3. Set aside.
4. Peel the pumpkin and chop it into small pieces.
5. Place in the baking dish and toss with the olive oil.
6. Increase the temperature to 390 degrees and cook the pumpkin for about 20 minutes.
7. Make sure to toss every 5 minutes or so.
8. Place the pumpkin in a serving: bowl.
9. Add baby spinach, radish and spring onion.
10. Toss with the vinegar.
11. Stir in the cubed blue cheese.
12. Top with the toasted pine nuts.

Eggplant Cheeseburger

(Prep + Cook Time: 10 minutes / Servings: 1)

Nutritional info per serving:

Calories 399, Carbohydrates 21 g, Fat 17 g, Protein 8 g

Ingredients:

1 hamburger bun

1 2-inch eggplant slice, cut along the round axis
1 mozzarella slice
Red onion cut into 3 rings

1 lettuce leaf
½ tbsp. tomato sauce
1 pickle, sliced

Directions:

1. Preheat the air fryer to 330 degrees F.
2. Place the eggplant slice and roast for 6 minutes.
3. Place the mozzarella slice on top of the eggplant and cook for 30 more seconds.
4. Spread the tomato sauce on one half of the bun.
5. Place the lettuce leaf on top of the sauce.
6. Place the cheesy eggplant on top of the lettuce.
7. Top with onion rings and pickles.
8. Top with the other bun half and enjoy.

Veggie Meatballs

(Prep + Cook Time: 30 minutes / Servings: 3)

Nutritional info per serving:

Calories 288, Carbohydrates 32 g, Fat 21 g, Protein 6 g

Ingredients:

2 tbsp. olive oil
2 tbsp. soy sauce
1 tbsp. flax meal
2 cups cooked chickpeas
½ cup sweet onion, diced
½ cup grated carrots

½ cup roasted cashews
Juice of 1 lemon
½ tsp. turmeric
1 tsp. cumin
1 tsp. garlic powder
1 cup rolled oats

Directions:

1. Preheat the air fryer to 350 degrees F.
2. Combine the oil, onions, and carrots into a baking dish and cook them in the air fryer for 5 minutes.
3. Meanwhile, ground the oats and cashews in a food processor.
4. Place them in a large bowl.
5. Process the chickpeas with the lemon juice and soy sauce, until smooth.
6. Add them to the bowl as well.
7. Add the onions and carrots to the bowl with the chickpeas.
8. Stir in all of the remaining ingredients, and mix until fully incorporated.
9. Make 12 meatballs out of the mixture.
10. Increase the temperature to 370 degrees.
11. Cook the meatballs for about 12 minutes.

Crunchy Parmesan Zucchini

(Prep + Cook Time: 40 minutes / Servings: 4)

Nutritional info per serving:

Calories 369, Carbohydrates 14 g, Fat 12 g, Protein 9.5 g

Ingredients:

4 small zucchini cut lengthwise
½ cup grated Parmesan cheese
½ cup breadcrumbs
¼ cup melted butter
¼ cup chopped parsley
4 garlic cloves, minced

Directions:

1. Preheat the air fryer to 350 degrees F.
2. In a bowl, mix the breadcrumbs, Parmesan, garlic, and parsley. Season with some salt and pepper, to taste. Stir in the melted butter.
3. Arrange the zucchinis with the cut side up.
4. Spread the mixture onto the zucchini evenly.
5. Place half of the zucchinis in the air fryer and cook for 13 minutes. Increase the temperature to 370 degrees F. Cook for 3 more minutes for extra crunchiness. Repeat with the other batch. Enjoy.

Chili Bean Burritos

(Prep + Cook Time: 30 minutes / Servings: 6))

Nutritional info per serving:

Calories 248, Carbohydrates 25 g, Fat 8.7 g, Protein 9 g

Ingredients:

6 tortillas
1 cup grated cheddar cheese
1 can (8 oz.) beans
1 tsp. seasoning, any kind

Directions:

1. Preheat the air fryer to 350 degrees F.
2. Mix the beans with the seasoning.
3. Divide the bean mixture between the tortillas.
4. Top the beans with cheddar cheese.
5. Roll the burritos and arrange them on a lined baking dish.
6. Place in the air fryer and cook for 5 minutes, or to your liking.
7. Serve as desired (I recommend salsa dipping) and enjoy.

Spinach and Feta Crescent Triangles

(Prep + Cook Time: 20 minutes / Servings: 4)

Nutritional info per serving:

Calories 178, Carbohydrates 10.8 g, Fat 11.9 g, Protein 8 g

Ingredients:

14 oz. store-bought crescent dough
1 cup steamed spinach
1 cup crumbled feta cheese
¼ tsp. garlic powder
1 tsp. chopped oregano
¼ tsp. salt

Directions:

1. Preheat the air fryer to 350 degrees F.
2. Roll the dough onto a lightly floured flat surface.
3. Combine the feta, spinach, oregano, salt, and garlic powder together in a bowl. Cut the dough into 4 equal pieces.
4. Divide the spinach/feta mixture between the dough pieces. Make sure to place the filling in the center.
5. Fold the dough and secure with a fork.
6. Place onto a lined baking dish, and then in the air fryer.
7. Cook for about 12 minutes, or until lightly browned.

Feta Cheese Triangles

(Prep + Cook Time: 20 minutes / Servings: 4)

Nutritional info per serving:

Calories 254, Carbohydrates 21 g, Fat 19 g, Protein 21 g

Ingredients:

4 oz. feta cheese
2 sheets filo pastry
1 egg yolk
2 tbsp. parsley, finely chopped

1 scallion, finely chopped
2 tbsp. of olive oil
salt and black pepper

Directions:

1. Inside a large bowl, beat the yolk and mix with the cheese, the chopped parsley and scallion.
2. Season with salt and black pepper .
3. Cut each filo sheet in three parts or strips.
4. Put a teaspoon of the feta mixture on the bottom.
5. Roll the strip in a spinning zigzag way until the filling of the inside mixture is completely wrapped in a triangle.
6. Preheat the Air Fryer to 360°F.
7. Brush the surface of the filo with a oil and place up to 5 triangles in the Air Frier's basket.
8. Cook for 5 minutes and lower the temperature to 330ºF.
9. Cook for 3 more minutes or until golden brown.

Cheesy Broccoli with Eggs

(Prep + Cook Time: 15 minutes / Servings: 4)

Nutritional info per serving:

Calories 265, Carbohydrates 19 g, Fat 23 g, Protein 26 g

Ingredients:

1 lb. of broccoli
4 eggs
1 cup cheese, shredded
1 cup cream
1 pinch nutmeg
1 tsp. ginger powder
salt and pepper

Directions:

1. Steam the broccoli for 5 minutes.
2. Then drain them and add 1 egg, cream, nutmeg, ginger, salt and pepper.
3. Butter several small ramekins and spread the mixture.
4. Sprinkle the shredded cheese on top.
5. Cook for 10 minutes at 250° F.

Eggplant Caviar

(Prep + Cook Time: 20 minutes / Servings: 3)

Nutritional info per serving:

Calories 125, Carbohydrates 12 g, Fat 3 g, Protein 2 g

Ingredients:

3 medium eggplants
½ red onion, chopped and blended
2 tbsp. balsamic vinegar
1 tbsp. olive oil
salt

Directions:

1. Preheat the Air Fryer.
2. Arrange the eggplants in a plate and cook them for 15 minutes at 380° F.
3. Remove them from the oven and let them cool down.
4. Then cut the eggplants in half, lengthwise, and empty their insides with a spoon.
5. Blend the onion in a blender.
6. Put the inside of the eggplants in the blender and process everything.
7. Add the vinegar, olive oil and salt, then blend again.
8. Serve cool with bread and tomato sauce or ketchup.

Ratatouille

(Prep + Cook Time: 30 minutes / Servings: 2)

Nutritional info per serving:

Calories 171, Carbohydrates 25.8 g, Fat 7.8 g, Protein 4.2 g

Ingredients:

1 tbsp. olive oil
3 roma tomatoes, thinly sliced
2 garlic cloves, minced
1 zucchini, thinly sliced
2 yellow bell peppers, sliced
1 tbsp. vinegar
2 tbsp. Herbs de Provence
Salt and pepper, to taste

Directions:

1. Preheat the air fryer to 390 degrees F.
2. Place all of the ingredients in a bowl. Season with some salt and pepper, and stir until the veggies are well coated.
3. Arrange the vegetable in a round baking dish and place in the air fryer.
4. Cook for about 15 minutes, shaking occasionally.
5. Let sit for 5 more minutes after the time goes off.

Chile Relleno

(Prep + Cook Time: 35 minutes / Servings: 4)

Nutritional info per serving:

Calories 269.3, Carbohydrates 35.3 g, Fat 15.5 g, Protein 23.8 g

Ingredients:

2 cans green chili peppers
1 cup cheddar cheese, shredded
1 cup Monterey Jack Cheese.
2 tbsp. all-purpose flour

2 large eggs, beaten
½ cup milk
1 can tomato sauce

Directions:

1. Preheat the Air Fryer to 380° F. Spray a baking dish with cooking spray.
2. Take half of the chilies and arrange them in the baking dish. Top the chilies with half of the cheese and cover with the other half of the chilies.
3. In a medium bowl, combine the eggs, the milk, the flour and pour the mixture over the chillies. Cook for 20 minutes.
4. Remove the chilies from the Air Fryer and pour the tomato sauce over them and cook for more 15 minutes. Remove from the Air Fryer and top with the remaining cheese.

Cabbage Steaks

(Prep + Cook Time: 25 minutes / Servings: 3)

Nutritional info per serving:

Calories 161, Carbohydrates 17.5 g, Fat 10 g, Protein 4.6 g

Ingredients:

1 cabbage head
1 tbsp. garlic stir-in paste

2 tbsp. olive oil
2 tsp. fennel seeds

Directions:

1. Preheat the air fryer to 350 degrees F.
2. Slice the cabbage into 1 ½-inch slices.
3. In a small bowl combine all of the other ingredients.
4. Brush the cabbage with the mixture.
5. Arrange the cabbage steaks in the air fryer and cook for 15 minutes.
6. Enjoy.

Vegetable Spring Rolls

(Prep + Cook Time: 15 minutes / Servings: 4)

Nutritional info per serving:

Calories 169.1, Carbohydrates 32.3 g, Fat 2.3 g, Protein 5.5 g

Ingredients:

- ½ cabbage, grated
- 2 carrots, grated
- 1 tsp. minced ginger
- 1 tsp. minced garlic
- 1 tsp. sesame oil
- 1 tsp. soy sauce
- 1 tsp. sesame seeds
- ½ tsp. salt
- 1 tsp. olive oil
- 1 package spring roll wrappers (8 to 10 wrappers)

Directions:

1. Preheat the air fryer to 370 degrees F.
2. Combine all of the ingredients in a large bowl.
3. Divide the mixture between the spring roll sheets, and roll them up.
4. Arrange on the baking mat. Cook in the air fryer for about 5 minutes.
5. Serve with your favorite dipping sauce and enjoy.

Cheesy Spinach Enchiladas

(Prep + Cook Time: 20 minutes / Servings: 4)

Nutritional info per serving:

Calories 356, Carbohydrates 43 g, Fat 27 g, Protein 21 g

Ingredients:

8 corn tortillas
2 cups shredded cheese
1 cup ricotta cheese
1 package frozen spinach
1 garlic clove, minced
½ cup of sliced onions
½ cup sour cream
1 tbsp. butter
1 can enchilada sauce

Directions:

1. In a saucepan, heat the oil and add garlic and onion. Cook until brown. Stir in the frozen spinach and keep cooking for 5 more minutes. Remove from the heat and stir in the ricotta cheese, keep stirring.
2. Add the sour cream and the shredded cheese. Warm the tortillas on low heat for about 15 seconds in the Air Fryer. Spoon ¼ cup of spinach mixture in the middle of a tortilla. Roll up and place seam side down in the Air Fryer's basket.
3. Pour the enchilada sauce over the tortillas and sprinkle with the remaining cheese. Cook for 15 minutes at 380° F.

Cheesy Muffins

(Prep + Cook Time: 8 minutes / Servings: 3)

Nutritional info per serving:

Calories 276, Carbohydrates 31 g, Fat 17 g, Protein 19 g

Ingredients:

3 split english muffins, toasted
1 cup cheddar cheese, smoked and shredded
1 mashed avocado

¼ cup ranch-style salad dressing
1 cup alfalfa sprouts
1 tomato, chopped
1 sweet onion, chopped
¼ cup sesame seeds, toasted

Directions:

1. Arrange the muffins open-faced in the Air Fryer's basket.
2. Spread the mashed avocado on each half of the muffin.
3. Place the halves close to each other. Cover the muffins with the sprouts, tomatoes, onion, dressing, sesame seeds and the cheese.
4. Cook for 7-8 minutes at 350° F.

Stuffed Garlicky Mushrooms

(Prep + Cook Time: 15 minutes / Servings: 2)

Nutritional info per serving:

Calories 116, Carbohydrates 19 g, Fat 11 g, Protein 5 g

Ingredients:

2 cups. small mushrooms
2 slices white bread
1 garlic clove, crushed
2 tsp. olive oil
1 tbsp. parsley, finely chopped
salt and black pepper

Directions:

1. Preheat the air fryer to 360°F.
2. In a food processor, grind the bread into very fine crumbs.
3. Then add the garlic, parsley and pepper. Mix and stir in the olive oil.
4. Cut off the mushroom stalks and fill the caps with the breadcrumbs.
5. Pat the crumbs inside the caps to ensure there are no loose crumbs.
6. Place the mushroom caps, one by one, inside the cooking basket and carefully slide them in the air fryer.
7. Cook for 10 minutes or until golden and crispy.

Stuffed Mushrooms

(Prep + Cook Time: 15 minutes / Servings: 3)

Nutritional info per serving:

Calories 111, Carbohydrates 12.3 g, Fat 3.8 g, Protein 8.9 g

Ingredients:

3 Portobello mushrooms
1 tomato, diced
1 small red onion, diced
1 green bell pepper, diced

½ cup grated mozzarella cheese
½ tsp. garlic powder
¼ tsp. pepper
¼ tsp. salt

Directions:

1. Preheat the air fryer to 330 degrees F. Wash the mushrooms, remove the stems, and pat them dry. Coat them with the olive oil.
2. Combine all of the remaining ingredients, except the mozzarella, in a small bowl. Divide the filling between the mushrooms.
3. Top the mushrooms with mozzarella. Place in the air fryer and cook for 8 minutes.

Cauliflower Rice

(Prep + Cook Time: 30 minutes / Servings: 4)

Nutritional info per serving:

Calories 137, Carbohydrates 19.7 g, Fat 4 g, Protein 10.2 g

Ingredients:

Tofu:

½ block tofu
½ cup diced onion
2 tbsp. soy sauce

1 tsp. turmeric
1 cup diced carrot

Cauliflower:

3 cups cauliflower rice (pulsed in a food processor)
2 tbsp. soy sauce
½ cup chopped broccoli
2 garlic cloves, minces

1 ½ tsp. toasted sesame oil
1 tbsp. minced ginger
½ cup frozen peas
1 tbsp. rice vinegar

Directions:

1. Preheat the air fryer to 370 degrees F. Crumble the tofu and combine it with all of the tofu ingredients. Place in a baking dish and air fry for 10 minutes.
2. Meanwhile, place all of the cauliflower ingredients in a large bowl. Mix to combine well. Add the cauliflower mixture to the tofu and stir to combine.
3. Cook for 12 minutes.

Air Fried Vegetables with Garlic

(Prep + Cook Time: 25 minutes / Servings: 6)

Nutritional info per serving:

Calories 176, Carbohydrates 21.7 g, Fat 9 g, Protein 12.2 g

Ingredients:

¾ lb. of green pepper
¾ lb. of tomatoes
1 medium onion

1 tbsp. of lemon juice
1 tbsp. of olive oil
1 tbsp. of coriander powder

Directions:

1. Preheat the Air Fryer to 360 degrees F. Line the peppers, the tomatoes and the onion in the Air Fryer's basket. Cook for 5 minutes, then flip around and cook for 5 more minutes. Remove them from the Air Fryer and peel their skin.
2. Place the vegetables in a blender and sprinkle with the salt and coriander powder. Blend to a smooth mixture and season with salt and olive oil.

Fish and Seafood Recipes

Frozen sesame Fish Fillets

(Prep + Cook Time: 20 minutes / Servings: 5)

Nutritional info per serving:

Calories 257.6, Carbohydrates 16.4 g, Fat 14 g, Protein 19.1 g

Ingredients:

5 frozen fish fillets
5 biscuits, crumbled
3 tbsp. flour
1 egg, beaten
Pinch of salt

Pinch of black pepper
¼ tsp. rosemary
3 tbsp. olive oil divided
A handful of sesame seeds

Directions:

1. Preheat the air fryer to 390 degrees F.
2. Combine the flour, pepper and salt, in a shallow bowl.
3. In another shallow bowl, combine the sesame seeds, crumbled biscuits, oil, and rosemary.
4. Dip the fish fillets into the flour mixture first, then into the beaten egg, and finally, coat them with the sesame mixture.
5. Arrange them inside the air fryer on a sheet of aluminum foil.
6. Cook the fish for 8 minutes.
7. Flip the fillets over and cook for additional 4 minutes.
8. Serve and enjoy.

Air Fried Dilly Salmon

(Prep + Cook Time: 30 minutes / Servings: 3)

Nutritional info per serving:

Calories 386, Carbohydrates 27 g, Fat 31 g, Protein 38 g

Ingredients:

3 pieces salmon, 5-6 oz. each

3 tbsp. olive oil

Dill Sauce:

½ cup greek yogurt
½ cup sour cream

2 tbsp. finely chopped dill
1 pinch salt

Directions:

1. Preheat the Air Fryer to 300° F. Drizzle the salmon with oil and season with a pinch of salt. Place the seasoned salmon into the Air Fryer's cooking basket.
2. Cook for 20 minutes and top with the dill sauce before serving.
3. For the dill sauce, in a large bowl, mix the yogurt, the sour cream, the chopped dill and salt.

Air Fried Calamari

(Prep + Cook Time: 130 minutes / Servings: 3)

Nutritional info per serving:

Calories 317.6, Carbohydrates 43.4 g, Fat 28 g, Protein 21.3 g

Ingredients:

½ lb. calamari rings
½ cup cornmeal or cornstarch
2 large eggs, beaten

2 mashed garlic cloves
1 cup of breadcrumbs
lemon juice

Directions:

1. Coat the calamari rings with the cornmeal.
2. The first mixture is prepared by mixing the eggs and the garlic.
3. Dip the calamari in the eggs' mixture. Then dip them in the breadcrumbs.
4. Put the calamari rings in the fridge for 2 hours to cool.
5. Then, line them in the Air Fryer and add oil generously.
6. Fry for 10-12 minutes at 390° F.
7. Serve with garlic mayonnaise and top with lemon juice.

Flatten Salmon Balls

(Prep + Cook Time: 13 minutes / Servings: 2)

Nutritional info per serving:

Calories 312, Carbohydrates 21 g, Fat 28.4 g, Protein 21 g

Ingredients:

4 oz. of tinned salmon
4 tbsp. celery, chopped
4 tbsp. spring onion, sliced
4 tbsp. wheat germ

4 tbsp. olive oil
1 large egg
1 tbsp. of dill, fresh and chopped
½ tsp. of garlic powder

Directions:

1. Preheat the Air Fryer to 390°F.
2. In a large bowl, mix the tinned salmon, egg, celery, onion, dill and garlic.
3. Shape the mixture into 2-inches size balls and roll them in wheat germ.
4. Heat the oil in a skillet and add the salmon balls.
5. Carefully flatten them. Then transfer them to the Air Fryer and fry for 8 minutes.
6. Serve with yogurt or mayonnaise.

Fish Tacos

(Prep + Cook Time: 15 minutes / Servings: 4)

Nutritional info per serving:

Calories 369, Carbohydrates 52 g, Fat 8.8 g, Protein 14.2 g

Ingredients:

4 corn tortillas
1 halibut fillet
2 tbsp. olive oil1
½ cup flour, divided

1 can of beer
4 tbsp. peach salsa
4 tsp. chopped cilantro
1 tsp. baking powder

Directions:

1. Preheat the air fryer to 390 degrees F. Combine 1 cup of flour, baking, powder and salt. Pour in some of the beer, enough to form a batter-like consistency. Save the rest of the beer to gulp with the taco.
2. Slice the fillet into 4 strips and toss them in half cup of flour.
3. Dip them into the beer batter and arrange on a lined baking sheet. Place in the air fryer and cook for 8 minutes. Meanwhile, spread the peach salsa on the tortillas. Top each tortilla with one fish strip and 1 tsp. chopped cilantro.

Sautéed Shrimp

(Prep + Cook Time: 10 minutes / Servings: 4)

Nutritional info per serving:

Calories 215, Carbohydrates 17 g, Fat 11 g, Protein 28 g

Ingredients:

5-6 oz. tiger shrimp, 12 to 16 pieces
1 tbsp. of olive oil
½ a tbsp. old bay seasoning

¼ a tbsp. cayenne pepper
¼ a tbsp. smoked paprika
1 pinch sea salt

Directions:

1. Preheat the Air Fryer to 380°F.
2. Mix the ingredients in a large mixing bowl.
3. Coat the shrimp with a little bit of oil and spices.
4. Place the shrimp in the Air Fryer's basket and fry for around 6-7 minutes.
5. Serve with rice or salad.
6. Enjoy.

Peppery and Lemony Haddock

(Prep + Cook Time: 15 minutes / Servings: 4)

Nutritional info per serving:

Calories 310.6, Carbohydrates 26.9 g, Fat 6.3 g, Protein 34.8 g

Ingredients:

4 haddock fillets
1 cup breadcrumbs
2 tbsp. lemon juice
½ tsp. black pepper
¼ cup dry instant potato flakes

1 egg, beaten
¼ cup Parmesan cheese
3 tbsp. flour
¼ tsp. salt

Directions:

1. Combine the flour, pepper and salt, in a small shallow bowl.
2. In another bowl, combine the lemon, breadcrumbs, Parmesan, and potato flakes.
3. Dip the fillets in the flour first, then in the beaten egg, and coat them with the lemony crumbs.
4. Arrange on a lined sheet and place in the air fryer.
5. Air fry for about 8 to 10 minutes at 370 degrees F.
6. Enjoy.

Soy Sauce Glazed Cod

(Prep + Cook Time: 15 minutes / Servings: 1)

Nutritional info per serving:

Calories 148, Carbohydrates 2.9 g, Fat 5.8 g, Protein 21 g

Ingredients:

1 cod fillet
1 tsp. olive oil
Pinch of sea salt
Pinch of pepper

1 tbsp. soy sauce
Dash of sesame oil
¼ tsp. ginger powder
¼ tsp. honey

Directions:

1. Preheat the air fryer to 370 degrees F.
2. Combine the olive oil, salt and pepper, and brush that mixture over the cod.
3. Place the cod onto an aluminum sheet and into the air fryer.
4. Cook for about 6 minutes.
5. Meanwhile, combine the soy sauce, ginger, honey, and sesame oil. Brush the glaze over the cod. Flip the fillet over and cook for additional 3 minutes.

Salmon Cakes

(Prep + Cook Time: 1 hour 15 minutes / Servings: 4)

Nutritional info per serving:

Calories 240.8, Carbohydrates 28.6 g, Fat 6.4 g, Protein 17.7 g

Ingredients:

10 oz. cooked salmon
14 oz. boiled and mashed potatoes
2 oz. flour
Handful capers

Handful chopped parsley
1 tsp. olive oil
Zest of 1 lemon

Directions:

1. Place the mashed potatoes in a large bowl and flake the salmon over.
2. Stir in capers, parsley, and lemon zest.
3. Shape small cakes out of the mixture.
4. Dust them with flour and place in the fridge to set, for about 1 hour.
5. Preheat the air fryer to 350 degrees F.
6. Brush the olive oil over the basket's bottom and add the cakes.
7. Cook for about 7 minutes.

Rosemary Garlic Prawns

(Prep + Cook Time: 1 h 15 minutes / Servings: 2)

Nutritional info per serving:

Calories 152.2, Carbohydrates 1.5 g, Fat 2.9 g, Protein 0.3 g

Ingredients:

8 large prawns
3 garlic cloves, minced
1 rosemary sprig, chopped

½ tbsp. melted butter
Salt and pepper, to taste

Directions:

1. Combine the garlic, butter, rosemary, and some salt and pepper, in a bowl.
2. Add the prawns to the bowl and mix to coat them well.
3. Cover the bowl and refrigerate for about an hour.
4. Preheat the air fryer to 350 degrees F.
5. Cook for about 6 minutes.
6. Increase the temperature to 390 degrees, and cook for one more minute.

Dessert Recipes

Soft Buttermilk Biscuits

(Prep + Cook Time: 25 minutes / Servings: 4)

Nutritional info per serving:

Calories 319.5, Carbohydrates 47.2 g, Fat 11.9 g, Protein 6.4 g

Ingredients:

1 ¼ cups all-purpose flour, plus some for dusting
½ tsp. baking soda
½ cup cake flour
¾ tsp. salt
½ tsp. baking powder
4 tbsp. butter, chopped
1 tsp. sugar
¾ cup buttermilk

Directions:

1. Preheat the air fryer to 400 degrees F.
2. Combine all of the dry ingredients, in a bowl.
3. Place the chopped butter into the bowl, and rub it into the flour mixture, until crumbed.
4. Stir in the buttermilk.
5. Flour a flat and dry surface and roll out until half-inch thick.
6. Cut out 10 rounds with a small cookie cutter.
7. Arrange the biscuits on a lined baking sheet.
8. Cook for 8 minutes.
9. Enjoy.

Orange Sponge Cake

(Prep + Cook Time: 50 minutes / Servings: 6)

Nutritional info per serving:

Calories 187, Carbohydrates 36.4 g, Fat 2.7 g, Protein 4.6 g

Ingredients:

9 oz. sugar
9 oz. self-rising flour
9 oz. butter
3 eggs

1 tsp. baking powder
1 tsp. vanilla extract
Zest of 1 orange

Frosting:

4 egg whites
Juice of 1 orange
1 tsp. orange food coloring

Zest of 1 orange
7 oz. superfine sugar

Directions:

1. Preheat the air fryer to 160 degrees F.
2. Place all of the cake ingredients in a bowl and beat with an electric mixer.
3. Transfer half of the batter into a prepared cake pan.
4. Bake for 15 minutes.
5. Repeat the process for the other half of the batter.
6. Meanwhile, prepare the frosting by beating all of the frosting ingredients together.
7. Spread the frosting mixture on top of one cake.
8. Top with the other cake.

Lemon Glazed Muffins

(Prep + Cook Time: 30 minutes / Servings: 6)

Nutritional info per serving:

Calories 235.9, Carbohydrates 43 g, Fat 6 g, Protein 3.7 g

Ingredients:

1 cup flour	¼ tsp. baking soda
½ cup sugar	½ tsp. salt
1 small egg	2 tbsp. vegetable oil
1 tsp. lemon zest	½ cup milk
¾ tsp. baking powder	½ tsp. vanilla extract

Glaze:

½ cup powdered sugar	2 tsp. lemon Juice

Directions:

1. Preheat the air fryer to 350 degrees F.
2. Combine all of the dry muffin ingredients, in a bowl.
3. In another bowl, whisk together the wet ingredients.
4. Gently combine the two mixtures.
5. Divide the batter between 6 greased muffin tins.
6. Place the muffin tins in the air fryer and cook for 12 to 14 minutes.
7. Meanwhile whisk the powdered sugar with the lemon juice.
8. Spread the glaze over the muffins.
9. Enjoy.

Mock Cherry Pie

(Prep + Cook Time: 30 minutes / Servings: 8)

Nutritional info per serving:

Calories 325, Carbohydrates 49.8 g, Fat 13.8 g, Protein 2.5 g

Ingredients:

2 store-bought pie crusts
21 oz. cherry pie filling

1 egg yolk
1 tbsp. milk

Directions:

1. Preheat the Air fryer to 310 degrees F. Place one piecrust in a pie pan.
2. Poke holes into the crust. Bake for about 5 minutes.
3. Spread the pie filling over. Cut the other piecrust into strips and arrange the pie-style over the baked crust.
4. Whisk the milk and egg yolk and brush the mixture over the pie.
5. Return the pie to the air fryer and bake for 15 minutes.

Simple Coffee Cake

(Prep + Cook Time: 30 minutes / Servings: 2)

Nutritional info per serving:

Calories 418.7, Carbohydrates 44.8 g, Fat 25.5 g, Protein 5.1 g

Ingredients:

¼ cup butter
½ tsp. instant coffee
1 tbsp. black coffee, brewed
1 egg
¼ cup sugar
¼ cup flour

1 tsp. cocoa powder
Pinch of salt
Powdered sugar, for icing

Directions:

1. Preheat the air fryer to 330 degrees F. Grease and small ring cake pan.
2. Beat the sugar and egg together in a bowl.
3. Beat in cocoa, instant coffee and black coffee. Stir in salt and flour.
4. Transfer the batter to the prepared pan.
5. Bake for about 15 minutes.

Berry Crumble

(Prep + Cook Time: 30 minutes / Servings: 6)

Nutritional info per serving:

Calories 261, Carbohydrates 42.7 g, Fat 9.6 g, Protein 2.6 g

Ingredients:

12 oz. fresh strawberries
7 oz. fresh raspberries
5 oz. fresh blueberries
5 tbsp. cold butter
2 tbsp. lemon juice

1 cup flour
½ cup sugar
1 tbsp. water
Pinch of salt

Directions:

1. Gently mass the berries, but make sure there are chunks left.
2. Mix the berries with the lemon juice and 2 tbsp. of the sugar.
3. Place the berry mixture at the bottom of a prepared round cake.
4. Combine the flour with the salt and sugar, in a bowl.
5. Add the water and rub the butter with your fingers until the mixture becomes crumbled.
6. Arrange the crumbly batter over the berries.
7. Cook in the air fryer at 390 degrees F for 20 minutes.
8. Enjoy.

Banana Fritters

(Prep + Cook Time: 15 minutes / Servings: 8)

Nutritional info per serving:

Calories 203, Carbohydrates 36.5 g, Fat 6.3 g, Protein 3.4 g

Ingredients:

8 bananas
3 tbsp. vegetable oil
3 tbsp. corn flour

1 egg white
¾ cup breadcrumbs

Directions:

1. Preheat the air fryer to 350 degrees F.
2. Combine the oil and breadcrumbs in a small bowl.
3. Coat the bananas with the corn flour first, brush them with egg white, and dip them in the breadcrumb mixture.
4. Arrange on a lined baking sheet and bake for about 8 minutes.

Baked apples

(Prep + Cook Time: 13 minutes / Servings: 2)

Nutritional info per serving:

Calories 483.3, Carbohydrates 76.5 g, Fat 21.8 g, Protein 8.1 g

Ingredients:

4 apples
1 oz. butter
2 oz. breadcrumbs
Zest of 1 orange

2 tbsp. chopped hazelnuts
2 oz. mixed seeds
1 tsp. cinnamon
2 tbsp. brown sugar

Directions:

1. Preheat the air fryer to 350 degrees. Core the apples.
2. Make sure to also score their skin in order to prevent them from splitting.
3. Combine the remaining ingredients in a bowl.
4. Stuff the apples with the mixture. Bake for 10 minutes.
5. Serve topped with chopped hazelnuts.

Pecan Pie

(Prep + Cook Time: 1 hour 10 minutes / Servings: 4)

Nutritional info per serving:

Calories 410, Carbohydrates 53 g, Fat 21.6 g, Protein 6.1 g

Ingredients:

¾ cup maple syrup
2 eggs
½ tsp. salt
¼ tsp. nutmeg
½ tsp. cinnamon
2 tbsp. almond butter

2 tbsp. brown sugar
½ cup chopped pecans
1 tbsp. butter, melted
1 8-inch pie dough
¾ tsp. vanilla extract

Directions:

1. Preheat the air fryer to 370 degrees F. Coat the pecans with the melted butter. Place the pecans into the air fryer and toast them for 10 minutes.
2. Place the piecrust into an 8-inch round pie pan, and place the pecans over.
3. Whisk together all of the remaining ingredients, in a bowl.
4. Pour the maple mixture over the pecans.
5. Set the temperature of the air fryer to 320 degrees F.
6. Bake the pie for about 25 minutes.
7. Serve as desired (I highly recommend vanilla ice cream) and enjoy.

Made in the USA
San Bernardino, CA
29 October 2018